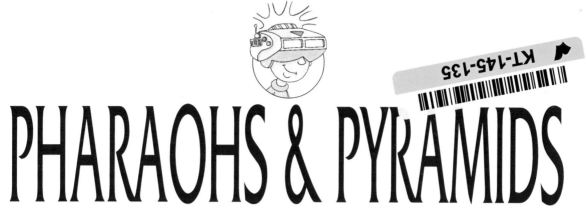

PHARAOHS & PYRAMIDS

Tony Allan
Edited by Philippa Wingate
Historical consultant: Vivienne Henry

Designed by Michele Busby and John Jamieson
Series designer: Russell Punter

Illustrated by Toni Goffe
Cover illustration by Stephen Cartwright

Contents

GOING BACK IN TIME

There are plenty of ways of going back in time. You do it every time you go to a museum or a castle and try to imagine how people used to live years ago. You can do it by looking at pictures and books too.

This book takes you on a trip back in time to the land of Ancient Egypt. The Ancient Egyptians were among the first to leave behind pictures and writings showing how they lived. It is by looking at these

things that we know what Ancient Egypt was like.

You will travel back nearly 3,400 years. This takes you to a time 1,400 years before Jesus was born. Dates before Jesus are written like this: 1400 BC.

1. THE TIME HELMET

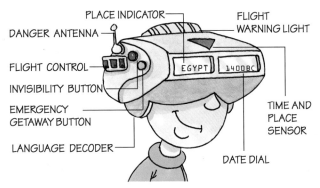

The magic time travel helmet has lots of useful gadgets, such as a language decoder, an invisiblity button and a button that takes you back home.

2. PICK A DESTINATION

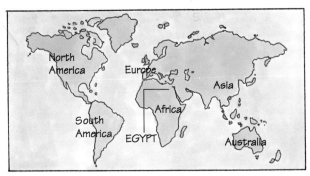

Set the helmet's controls to "Egypt" in "1400 BC". Below are a few stop-off points that show how things change when you jump back in time.

3. GO!

This is northwest Europe in 1940. Notice that both the plane and the radio look different and there is no television, because most families didn't have one.

Another 40 years back in time things are quite a bit different. There is no electricity, lots of decorations, and the women wear long skirts.

If you make a big jump of 400 years, you will find that the only lighting is by candles, and there's a big open fire. Most of the furniture is plain, and the window is made of tiny panes of glass.

This time you have moved back in time and place to Rome in the year 100. You have gone back nearly 2,000 years now, but you still have almost as far to go again. Next stop Ancient Egypt!

THE PEOPLE YOU WILL MEET

All Egyptians live within a few miles of a river called the Nile. The weather is warm and sunny most of the time, so they don't need to wear many clothes. Children hardly ever wear anything at all.

Rich people have pleasant lives. They have servants and slaves to do much of the work. But most of the people in Egypt are poor peasants who have to work hard to live.

The Vizier is Pharaoh's chief helper. It is his job to see that Pharaoh's orders are carried out.

Most Egyptians are peasants. They have to grow enough food to live on, and pay taxes to Pharaoh's officials. If they fail to pay they are beaten.

Priests work in the temples, looking after the gods. To keep themselves pure and clean, they bathe four times a day, shave their bodies, and dress in the finest white linen.

Pharaoh is the ruler of all Egypt. His subjects believe that he is a god in the body of a man. They think that he can do no wrong.

Soldiers lead hard, dangerous lives. But a few successful ones may become rich and famous generals.

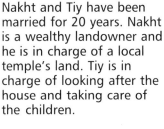

Most servants are free to leave their masters if they want, but others are slaves. Slaves are usually foreigners who were captured in wars.

NAKHT AND HIS FAMILY

The main people you will meet in this book are Nakht and his family. They live in a big house on the Nile near a city named Memphis.

NAKHT

TIY

Nakht and Tiy have been married for 20 years. Nakht is a wealthy landowner and he is in charge of a local temple's land. Tiy is in charge of looking after the house and taking care of the children.

MOSI

Mosi, the eldest son, is 16. Nakht wanted him to work in the temple, but Mosi wants to be a soldier. Nakht has finally agreed to this, and has promised to introduce him to a general he knows.

SHERY

Shery, the eldest daughter, is 13. Because she is a girl, she doesn't go to school. Instead she is taught what she needs to know at home. This includes singing and dancing.

HORI

Hori, the youngest son, is 10. He goes to a school in a temple in Memphis, where he learns to read and write. He expects to take over his father's job after Nakht has retired.

MEU

The youngest daughter is called Meu, which means "kitten". She is 8 years old. After her lessons, she spends most of the day playing outside in the sunshine.

AHMOSE

Ahmose, Nakht's nephew, is staying with his uncle's family. His own father has gone on a long trading voyage to Byblos, a port across the Mediterranean Sea in Lebanon.

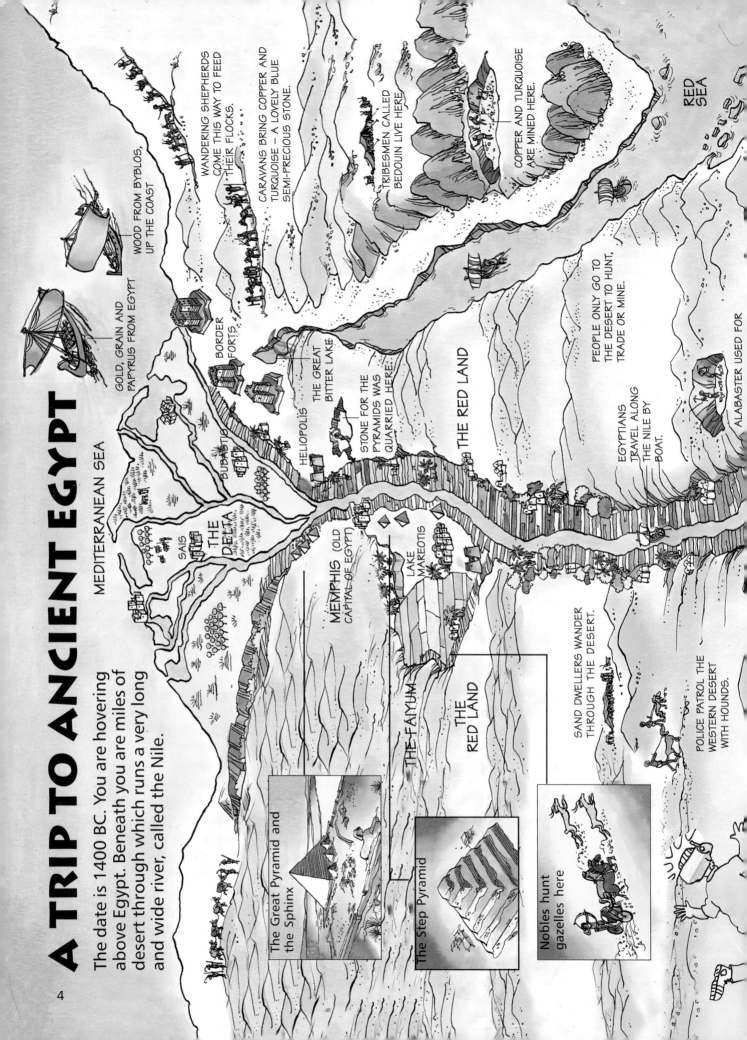

A TRIP TO ANCIENT EGYPT

The date is 1400 BC. You are hovering above Egypt. Beneath you are miles of desert through which runs a very long and wide river, called the Nile.

WOOD FROM BYBLOS, UP THE COAST

WANDERING SHEPHERDS COME THIS WAY TO FEED THEIR FLOCKS.

CARAVANS BRING COPPER AND TURQUOISE – A LOVELY BLUE SEMI-PRECIOUS STONE.

TRIBESMEN CALLED BEDOUIN LIVE HERE

COPPER AND TURQUOISE ARE MINED HERE.

RED SEA

GOLD, GRAIN AND PAPYRUS FROM EGYPT

BORDER FORTS

MEDITERRANEAN SEA

HELIOPOLIS

THE GREAT BITTER LAKE

STONE FOR THE PYRAMIDS WAS QUARRIED HERE.

THE RED LAND

PEOPLE ONLY GO TO THE DESERT TO HUNT, TRADE OR MINE.

EGYPTIANS TRAVEL ALONG THE NILE BY BOAT.

BUBASTIS

SAIS

THE DELTA

MEMPHIS (OLD CAPITAL OF EGYPT)

LAKE MAREOTIS

THE FAIYUM

THE RED LAND

ALABASTER USED FOR

SAND DWELLERS WANDER THROUGH THE DESERT.

POLICE PATROL THE WESTERN DESERT WITH HOUNDS.

The Great Pyramid and the Sphinx

The Step Pyramid

Nobles hunt gazelles here

4

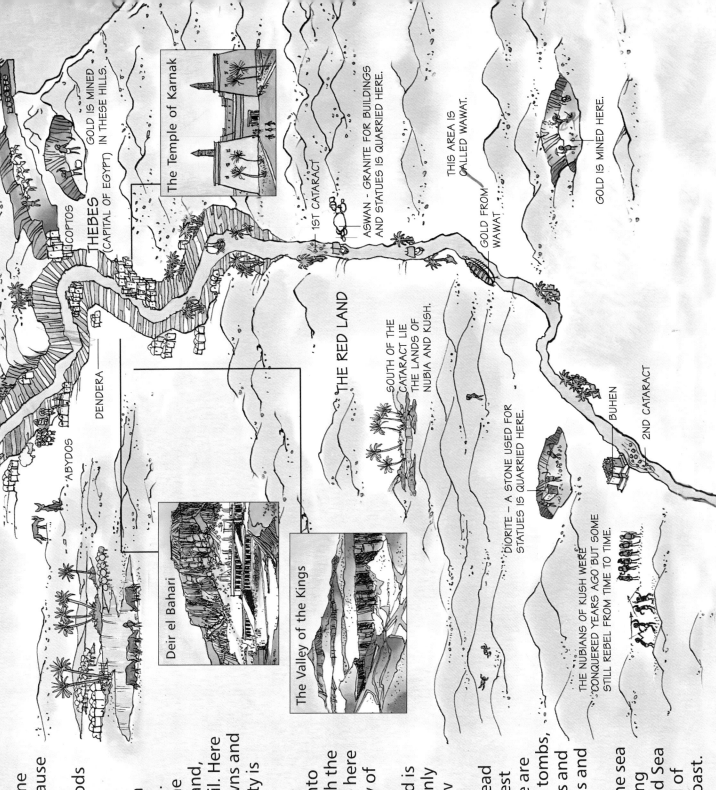

GOLD IS MINED IN THESE HILLS.

COPTOS

THEBES (CAPITAL OF EGYPT)

The Temple of Karnak

1ST CATARACT

ASWAN - GRANITE FOR BUILDINGS AND STATUES IS QUARRIED HERE.

THIS AREA IS CALLED WAWAT.

GOLD IS MINED HERE.

GOLD FROM WAWAT.

DENDERA

ABYDOS

THE RED LAND

SOUTH OF THE CATARACT LIE THE LANDS OF NUBIA AND KUSH.

Deir el Bahari

The Valley of the Kings

DIORITE – A STONE USED FOR STATUES IS QUARRIED HERE.

BUHEN

2ND CATARACT

THE NUBIANS OF KUSH WERE CONQUERED YEARS AGO BUT SOME STILL REBEL FROM TIME TO TIME.

Without the Nile, no one could live in Egypt because there is very little rain. Every year the river floods its banks. When the waters go down, they leave a strip of land on which crops grow well.

The Egyptians call the river valley the Black Land, because of its black soil. Here they build villages, towns and temples. The capital city is called Thebes.

In an area called the Delta, the river splits into many channels to reach the sea. Lots of people live here because there is plenty of water.

The desert all around is called the Red Land. Only wild animals and a few people live there. The Egyptians bury their dead in the desert on the west bank of the Nile. There are great monuments and tombs, including the pyramids and the Valleys of the Kings and Queens.

The Egyptians call the sea the Great Green. Trading ships sail down the Red Sea to the mysterious land of Punt, on the African coast.

5

ALONG THE NILE

It is late in the year and the farmers are busy sowing seeds for next year's harvest.

Another urgent job is to repair the canal banks. Canals are used for travel and to carry water to fields far from the Nile.

There is very little rain, so water can't be wasted. Large pools called catch-basins are built to store flood water, so it can be used throughout the year to water the fields.

The Nile itself is busy with traffic. It is Egypt's main highway. Statues and stones for building are carried down the river in ships and barges.

Nakht's boat has just turned off the river. He is going home to his house.

STATUE OF PTAH FOR A TEMPLE

FISHERMEN IN BOATS MADE OF PAPYRUS REEDS

NAKHT'S BOAT IS MADE OF WOOD.

NAKHT

ROPE STRETCH REMEASURING THE FIELDS.

6

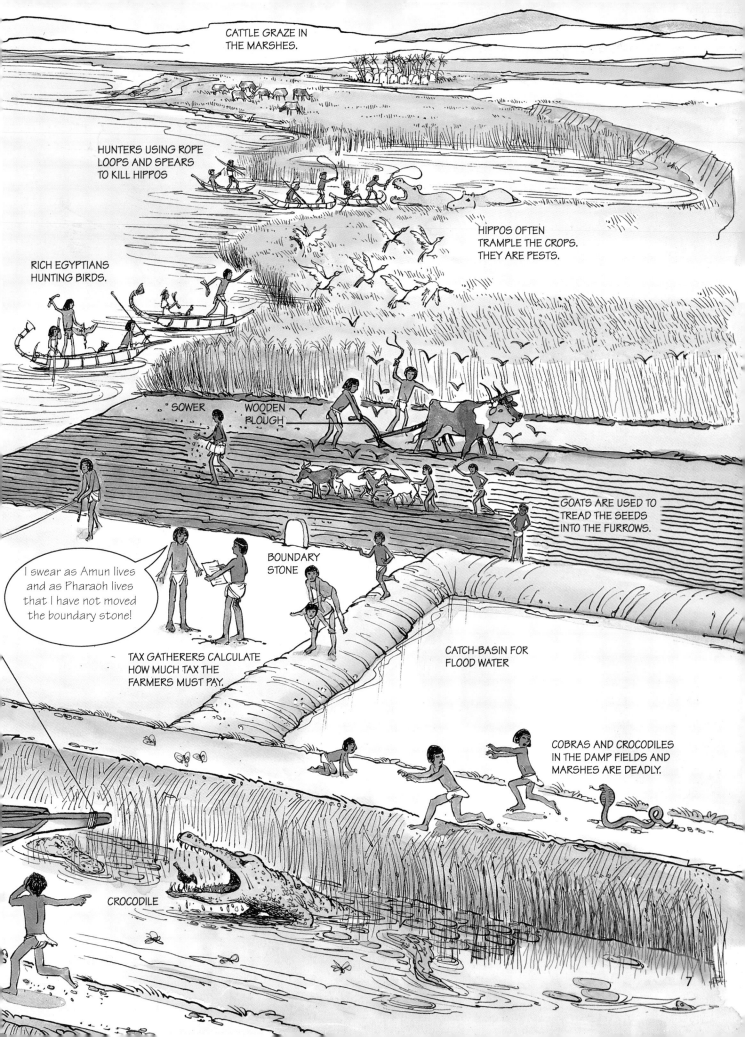

CATTLE GRAZE IN THE MARSHES.

HUNTERS USING ROPE LOOPS AND SPEARS TO KILL HIPPOS

HIPPOS OFTEN TRAMPLE THE CROPS. THEY ARE PESTS.

RICH EGYPTIANS HUNTING BIRDS.

SOWER

WOODEN PLOUGH

GOATS ARE USED TO TREAD THE SEEDS INTO THE FURROWS.

BOUNDARY STONE

I swear as Amun lives and as Pharaoh lives that I have not moved the boundary stone!

TAX GATHERERS CALCULATE HOW MUCH TAX THE FARMERS MUST PAY.

CATCH-BASIN FOR FLOOD WATER

COBRAS AND CROCODILES IN THE DAMP FIELDS AND MARSHES ARE DEADLY.

CROCODILE

AT HOME WITH NAKHT

Nakht lives with his family near the Nile. He owns a house, a stableyard and some small buildings where his servants live and where food is cooked.

Nakht has a lot of land around his house. Peasants farm this land, and in return they give Nakht some of the food they grow. A steward makes sure that the peasants give Nakht all that they owe him.

Nakht's house is built with bricks made of mud mixed with straw. Inside, the house is cool and shady, but the family spend a lot of time outdoors in the sunshine.

Nakht's slaves and gardeners look after the grounds around the house.

COLLECTING HONEY FROM BEEHIVES

NAKHT

TIY

PILLARED ROOM FOR RECEIVING NAKHT'S IMPORTANT GUESTS

WORKMEN PICK FIGS WITH THE HELP OF PET BABOONS.

THIS MAN DIDN'T BRING ENOUGH GEESE.

DUCKS' EGGS

NAKHT'S STEWARD

PEASANTS BRING CATTLE AND GEESE TO THE STEWARD.

8

NAKHT'S CHARIOT AND HORSES FOR HUNTING IN THE DESERT

GRAIN IS STORED IN HUTS MADE OF DRIED MUD.

GRINDING CORN

YOUNG CHILDREN KEEP COOL BY HAVING MOST OF THEIR HAIR SHAVED OFF.

HIGH WINDOWS LET IN AIR AND LIGHT.

MOSI AND HIS COUSIN AHMOSE ARE PLAYING A POPULAR BOARD GAME CALLED SENIT.

PAINTED WOODEN PILLARS

SERVANTS EMPTY THE TOILET BOWL INTO THE CANAL.

A WOODEN HEADREST

RAZOR

THE BED HAS A BASE OF LEATHER STRAPS ON A WOODEN FRAME.

THIS SERVANT IS PLUCKING GEESE.

A FEAST

Nakht is giving a feast to celebrate his return home. The Egyptians love parties.

The guests are gathered in the central hall of Nakht's house. Married couples sit together, but unmarried boys and girls have to sit apart.

Servants bring food and wine to the guests, while dancers and musicians entertain them. After the dancing, a harpist sings one of Egypt's oldest songs. The words tell people to make the most of their lives, because life is only a dream, and everyone will die one day.

THE GUESTS EAT THE FOOD WITH THEIR FINGERS AND THEN WASH THEM IN BOWLS OF WATER.

SOME GUESTS WEAR LOTUS BLOSSOMS IN THEIR HAIR.

SERVANTS OFFER FOOD AND POUR WINE.

PET GOOSE

PREPARING FOOD

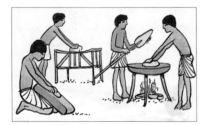

Nakht's servants are busy baking bread and a variety of cakes for the guests at the feast to enjoy.

Ducks and geese make popular meat courses. They are roasted over an open fire. The cook fans the flames to keep them burning.

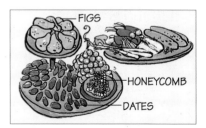

FIGS

HONEYCOMB

DATES

Vegetables and fruit, including figs, dates and grapes, are grown on Nakht's land. Honey is used to sweeten drinks and food.

SHERY GETS READY FOR THE FEAST

Holding her bronze mirror, Shery rims her eyes with a black powder called kohl.

She grinds red clay into a powder to rub on her cheeks and palms.

A servant helps Shery put on her wig. On top of it she places a cone of perfumed oil.

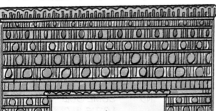

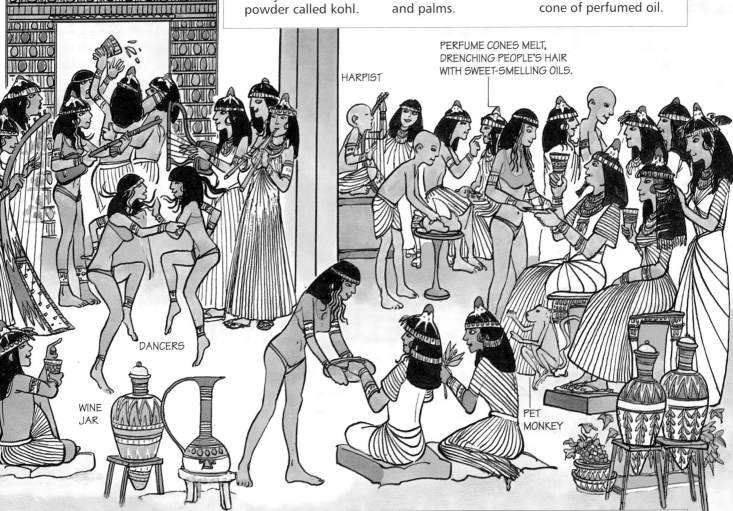

PERFUME CONES MELT, DRENCHING PEOPLE'S HAIR WITH SWEET-SMELLING OILS.

HARPIST

DANCERS

WINE JAR

PET MONKEY

MAKING WINE

Most Egyptians drink beer, but rich people are also fond of wine. Landowners often grow grapes on trellises like these.

The grapes are taken to the press. While some workers trample them underfoot, others collect the juice that gushes out.

The juice is poured into pottery jars to ferment into wine. These are sealed with a cap of mud and leaves which dry in the sun.

VISITING A TEMPLE

The temple in which Nakht works is like a small city. It has workshops, a school, a library, storerooms and granaries. Outside its walls, there are acres of farmland that belong to the temple.

The Egyptians believe that temples are the homes of gods. The most important part of a temple is a small room that only priests enter.

It is the sanctuary where the god lives.

Ordinary people are not allowed into the sanctuary. They can go to the temple to make offerings to the god or to work.

Today, Hori has come to learn how to read and write at the temple school.

A votive tablet. People buy them to offer to the gods, hoping the gods will listen to their prayers.

CHIEF PRIEST'S HOUSE

SACRED LAKE, WHERE PRIESTS BATHE BEFORE CEREMONIES

FLAGPOLE

THE HYPOSTYLE HALL HAS BIG PILLARS.

STATUE OF PHARAOH

HORI

AN OBELISK. ITS TOP IS COVERED WITH GOLD.

MAKING AN OFFERING

THESE TOWERS FORM A GATEWAY CALLED A PYLON.

SETTING UP BOOTHS FOR A TEMPLE FESTIVAL

SONS OF TEMPLE OFFICIALS LEARN TO READ AND WRITE.

THE GODS OF EGYPT

The Egyptians believe in many different gods. All Egyptians worship the great gods, like Amun. But each city has a god of its own, who lives in the local temple.

Here are three gods that all Egyptians worship.

Amun of Thebes was the king of the gods

Ptah, the god of Memphis, and the god of craftsmen

Bes, a dwarf god, brings luck and happiness at home.

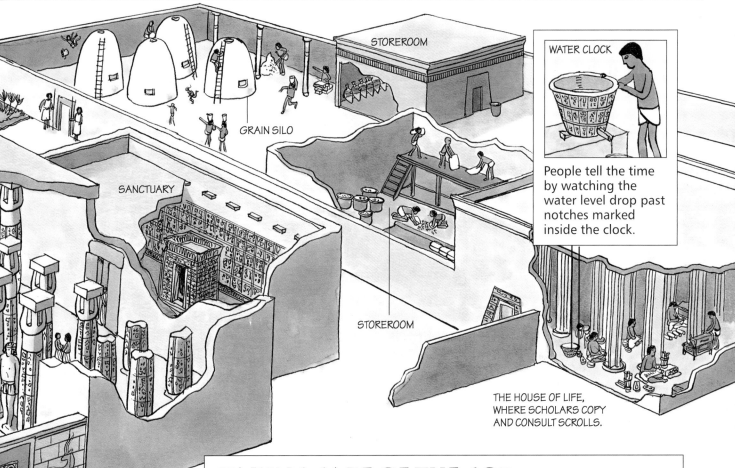

STOREROOM

GRAIN SILO

SANCTUARY

STOREROOM

WATER CLOCK

People tell the time by watching the water level drop past notches marked inside the clock.

THE HOUSE OF LIFE, WHERE SCHOLARS COPY AND CONSULT SCROLLS.

MUSICIANS ...ING THEIR ...TRUMENTS

SCHOOLROOM

TAKING CARE OF THE GOD

Each morning a priest, who has just shaved and washed, enters the sanctuary. It is his job to look after the god.

He takes the god's statue out of its shrine. He sprinkles water on it, changes its clothing and then offers it food and drink.

Finally, he puts it back in the shrine and leaves the doors open until evening. As he goes out, he wipes away his footprints.

GOING TO SCHOOL

Most Egyptian children never go to school. As soon as they are old enough, the boys go to work with their fathers and the girls are taught how to run a home.

Hori goes to school because he wants to be a scribe at the temple, like his father Nakht. A scribe is someone who is specially trained to read and write.

Today, Hori and his schoolfriends are writing on pieces of stone or broken pottery called *ostraca*. The brushes they use to sketch writing symbols are made from reeds.

Hori doesn't like school much. There are no sports or games, and the teacher is very strict. Sometimes he beats lazy pupils with his cane. But Nakht tells Hori that if he studies, he will become wise, rich and successful.

A CASE CONTAINING SCROLLS OF A KIND OF PAPER CALLED PAPYRUS

HORI HARD AT WORK

CANE

WATER JUG

INKSTAND

REED BRUSH

RAG FOR ERASING MISTAKES

OSTRACA

MAKING PAPYRUS

The Egyptians use papyrus reeds to make paper. The reeds grow in marshy ground. Workers cut them down and carry them away to a workshop.

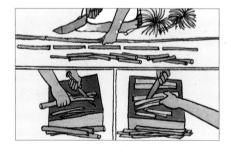

First, the long reeds are chopped into short lengths. Then the green outer skin is peeled away. The white pith inside is cut lengthways into wafer-thin slices.

MALLET FOR BEATING

CLOTH

POLISHING STONE

Two layers of pith are placed crossways on a block. A man places a cloth over them, and beats them into flat sheets. The sheets are polished smooth with a stone.

EGYPTIAN WRITING

HIERATIC

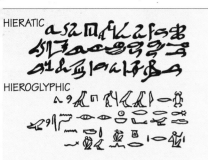

HIEROGLYPHIC

WORD SIGNS

OLD MAN

JACKAL

SUN

HILL/FOREIGN LANDS

SOUND SIGNS

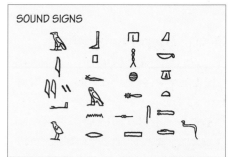

The Egyptians have two kinds of writing – hieratic and hieroglyphic. Hieratic is a kind of shorthand, used for day-to-day business. Hieroglyphic writing is used for religious writings and inscriptions on monuments. It is very difficult to learn.

Hori will be a temple scribe, so he has to learn hieroglyphic writing. Hieroglyphic writing is already about 2,000 years old. At first it was a picture language with a drawing for each word. A little drawing of a boat meant "boat".

Later, signs were used to stand for sounds, as the letters in our alphabet do. Words could be made up of several different signs. The picture above shows the main sound signs, but other signs are also used for groups of letters.

LEARNING TO READ HIEROGLYPHS

Hori spends a lot of time at school studying hieroglyphic writing, to learn how to read the language. The writing shown above is a mixture of sound signs and word signs.

The Egyptians have no written vowels, so many words look alike. To help tell them apart, they often write the sound of a word, then put a special sign, called a determinative, after it to make its meaning clearer.

This is what the writing shown above means:

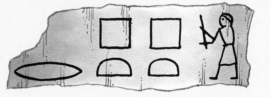

The word for "house" sounds like the word for "go forth", so the house symbol is used for both. The walking legs show that here it means "go forth".

The club is a sound sign which means "majesty". The snake is the Egyptian letter "f". But it can also be used to mean "his", as it does here.

The mouth is the sound sign for "r" and, also, the word for "to". The stool is the sound sign for "p", and the loaf of bread is the sign for "t". Repeated, they spell the word for "crush". To make the meaning of the word even clearer, a determinative sign for "force" – a man with a stick – is added on at the end.

As Egypt is flat, the sign for "hill" also means "foreign land". Here it is plural. So the sentence reads: "Goes forth His Majesty to crush foreign lands."

KEY   WORD SIGNS AND DETERMINATIVES   SOUND SIGNS

 (WALKING LEGS) GO

 (MAN WITH STICK) FORCE

 (HILLS) FOREIGN LAND

(HOUSE) STANDS FOR "PR"

(CLUB) STANDS FOR "HM"

(HORNED VIPER) STANDS FOR "F"

(MOUTH) STANDS FOR "R"

 (STOOL) STANDS FOR "P"

(LOAF OF BREAD) STANDS FOR "T"

A TRIP TO THE PYRAMIDS

The pyramids were built over a thousand years before Nakht was born. They are very old, but they still look magnificent. They stand on the edge of the desert, across the Nile from Nakht's home.

During the flood season the Nile rises close to the pyramids. Sightseers, like Nakht and his children, can sail up to them and pay their respects to the dead Pharaohs or visit the buildings.

HOW THE PYRAMIDS WERE BUILT

1. One way of cutting stone blocks for a pyramid was to cut notches in solid rock and hammer in wooden wedges. When water was poured on the wedges, they swelled, splitting off the blocks cleanly.

2. Most of the massive blocks used to build the Great Pyramid were quarried in the desert nearby. The white stones used to form the outer layer were brought across the Nile from the east bank.

3. The ground where the pyramid was to be built had to be cleared of sand and stones. Workers dug long channels and filled them with water. When the water didn't run to one end, they knew the site was level.

4. The most difficult job of all was to raise the heavy stones into place. Most people think the stones were pulled up a huge earth ramp that was raised each time a new layer of stones was added.

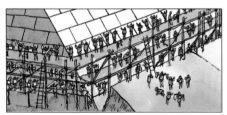

5. When the pyramid was finished, the ramp was taken away layer by layer. As the ramp went down, workers put white blocks of limestone on the jagged sides of the pyramid, to give them a smooth outer surface.

6. After many years' work, the pyramid was ready. When the Pharaoh died, his coffin was dragged up to the burial chamber inside it. Then the way into the pyramid was blocked with stone slabs and hidden.

INSIDE THE GREAT PYRAMID

The most impressive of all the pyramids is the Great Pyramid, built for Pharaoh Cheops. It is the biggest stone building ever built. Two million huge blocks of cut stone were used to construct it.

King Cheops had it made to keep his body safe after his death. He stocked the burial chamber with treasure to use in his afterlife.

Despite his efforts, thieves found their way in to the pyramid. There is nothing left inside the pyramid but the stone coffin in which Cheops was buried.

SMALL PYRAMIDS FOR THE PHARAOH'S CHIEF QUEENS WERE BUILT BESIDE THE TOMB.

THIS CAUSEWAY LINKS THE MORTUARY TEMPLE TO A SECOND TEMPLE NEARER THE NILE.

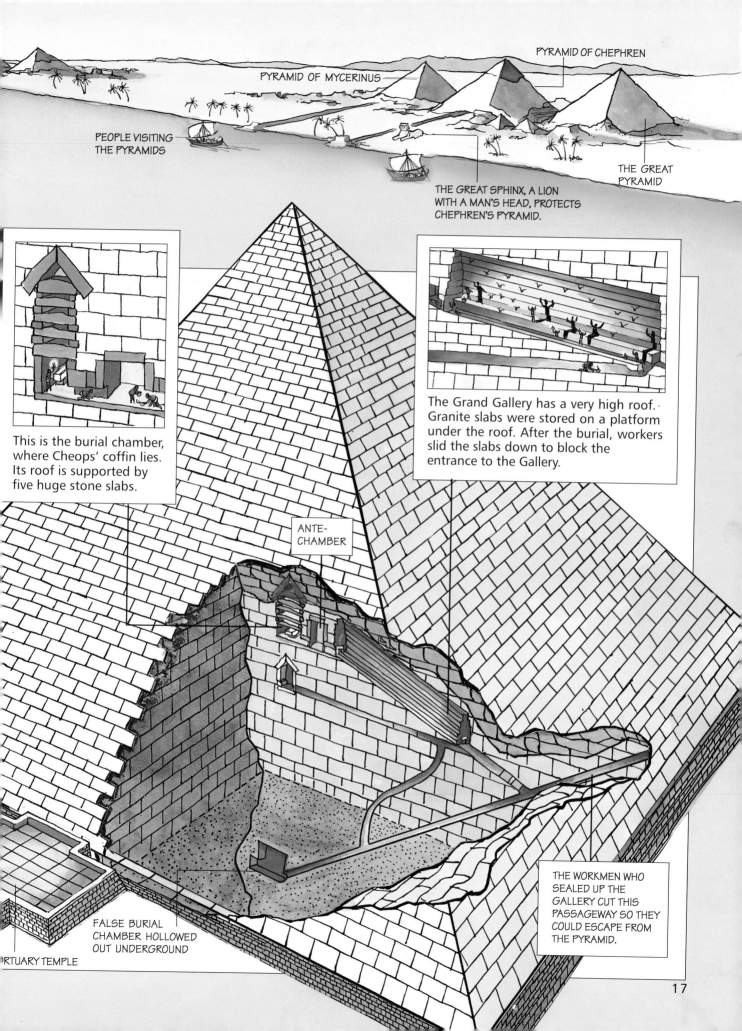

PYRAMID OF CHEPHREN

PYRAMID OF MYCERINUS

PEOPLE VISITING
THE PYRAMIDS

THE GREAT
PYRAMID

THE GREAT SPHINX, A LION
WITH A MAN'S HEAD, PROTECTS
CHEPHREN'S PYRAMID.

This is the burial chamber,
where Cheops' coffin lies.
Its roof is supported by
five huge stone slabs.

The Grand Gallery has a very high roof.
Granite slabs were stored on a platform
under the roof. After the burial, workers
slid the slabs down to block the
entrance to the Gallery.

ANTE-
CHAMBER

THE WORKMEN WHO
SEALED UP THE
GALLERY CUT THIS
PASSAGEWAY SO THEY
COULD ESCAPE FROM
THE PYRAMID.

FALSE BURIAL
CHAMBER HOLLOWED
OUT UNDERGROUND

RTUARY TEMPLE

17

SETTING SAIL FOR THEBES

Today, Mosi is catching a boat. He must sail to Thebes to join his father, Nakht, who is on business at Pharaoh's court.

At the port, a boat has just arrived with a precious cargo of goods from a land named Punt.

The port is very busy. Some men are unloading the boat, while others note down its cargo. People are shopping. There is no money, so they exchange goods. This is called bartering. A group of bedouins have come from the desert to trade.

LEATHER WORKERS

POOR PEOPLE LIVE IN SMALL, CRAMPED HOUSES.

MOSI

BARBER

STALL-KEEPERS ARE DOING GOOD BUSINESS.

SCALES

PEOPLE WORK OUTSIDE BECAUSE IT IS SO HOT.

A BEDOUIN MAN WITH A BEARD AND BRIGHT CLOTHES

BEDOUINS' DONKEYS LADEN WITH DYED CLOTH TO EXCHANGE FOR FOOD

BOAT FROM PUNT CARRYING A RICH CARGO

BABOONS

ELEPHANT TUSKS

N APPRENTICE
IXING CLAY

VENT TO
CATCH BREEZES

IN HOT WEATHER PEOPLE
SLEEP ON BEDROLLS ON
THE ROOFS.

KILN FOR
BAKING
POTS

POTTERS
AT WORK

HOUSES, POTS AND
JARS ARE MADE
FROM NILE MUD.

19

AT PHARAOH'S COURT

Nakht is attending a reception at Pharaoh's palace in Thebes.

Ambassadors have come from Syria, a mountainous land northeast of Egypt. They are bringing gifts to Pharaoh. Some of these will go to Nakht's temple for the god Ptah. The gifts include a bear for the royal zoo. The Syrians also bring royal children who will stay at court. They will be treated well, but they are hostages who will be killed if their parents rebel.

Like all Egyptians, Nakht worships Pharaoh. He believes that Pharaoh is the son of the god Amun and that his word is law.

Young Pharaoh sits with his wife in the audience-hall. He is bored with the Syrian's flattery. He has heard news of a revolt in Kush. He is awaiting the arrival of his governor from Kush. Pharaoh knows that if there has been a revolt it will mean war.

PHARAOH AND HIS WIFE SIT ON A RAISED PLATFORM.

SYRIAN AMBASSADORS

A DAY IN THE LIFE OF PHARAOH

Pharaoh is dressed by his servants. They give him objects that are symbols of his royalty, a flail, a crook, and a headdress called a *nemes*.

Every morning in the temple, Pharaoh burns incense over a gift that has been offered to Amun. He asks the god to bring Egypt good luck.

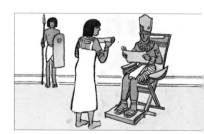

Much of the day is taken up governing the country. Pharaoh reads letters and consults his advisors. The Vizier helps to keep him informed.

THE CROWNS OF EGYPT

Pharaoh wears different crowns for different occasions. This is the blue war crown.

The White Crown is the crown of southern Egypt. The Red Crown is the crown of the Delta region.

As ruler of all Egypt, Pharaoh usually wears the Double Crown, which unites the Red and White.

The elaborate, top-heavy *hemhemet* crown is only worn for ceremonies at the temple.

COPPER

ROYAL CHILDREN

A TRUMPETER ANNOUNCESTHE GOVERNOR'S ARRIVAL.

THE GOVERNOR OF KUSH ARRIVING WITH TWO LOYAL PRINCES FROM NUBIA

NAKHT

n the afternoon, Pharaoh goes to watch work on a temple he is having built for himself. Workers are hauling huge stone blocks nto place.

Pharaoh loves hunting in the desert, but it can be dangerous. The fiercest prey are lions. In ten years Pharaoh has killed more than 100 lions.

Back in the palace, Pharaoh relaxes and plays a game of *senit* with his wife. The game is played on a board with 30 squares. Then Pharaoh goes to bed.

BATTLE!

The news from Kush is bad. Nubian tribesmen who live to the south of Egypt have rebelled. Pharaoh decides to send soldiers to punish them.

An expedition is organized quickly. Egypt has an army of trained soldiers. The most highly trained are charioteers, who provide their own chariots. Only a few of them will go to Kush, because it is difficult to carry horses down the Nile on boats.

One of the soldiers joining the expedition is Nakht's son Mosi. He is a new recruit and is eager to prove himself in battle.

1. PHARAOH CALLS HIS MEN TO ARMS

Bring out the weapons so that the courage of my father Amun may humble the rebellious lands!

SCRIBE

BOWS

QUIVERS

WAR COUNCIL

SPEARS

AXES

While the soldiers receive their weapons for the battle, Pharaoh encourages them with a traditional battle cry.

2. THE EXPEDITION CAMPS BY THE NILE

The journey to the battlefield takes many days. The army has made camp on the way. Generals have their own tents, but the soldiers sleep in the open.

GUARDS

SOLDIERS WRESTLING

CAMP BED

COOK

Soldiers have to work long hours and often go hungry. If they make mistakes, they are beaten. But if they fight bravely, Pharaoh may reward them with farmland and foreign slaves.

3. ATTACK!

Archers begin the attack with a hail of arrows, then foot soldiers run forward. The Nubians are no match for the better armed Egyptians.

The battle is soon over. Chariots chase the survivors from the field.

4. SPOILS OF VICTORY

Nubian captives are led away into slavery. To check how many of the enemy are dead, scribes count piles of hands cut from dead warriors.

The Egyptian soldiers set fire to the Nubian camp, and steal their food and animal skins.

A WARRIOR IS BURIED

During the battle in Kush, some Egyptian soldiers were killed. One was Mosi's friend named Bata.

Bata's parents have brought his body to Thebes for burial. The funeral procession makes its way to a tomb on the west bank of the Nile. Four priests perform a burial ceremony.

THE TOMB HAS BEEN HOLLOWED OUT OF A CLIFF.

WOMEN MOURNERS HOWL AND THROW DUST OVER THEIR HEADS.

THIS PRIEST WEARS THE MASK OF THE JACKAL-HEADED GOD ANUBIS.

FOOD AND WINE FOR THE FEAST HELD AFTER THE BURIAL

BATA'S BODY INSIDE A MUMMY

THIS CHEST HOLDS JARS CONTAINING PARTS OF THE DEAD MAN'S BODY.

SOME MOURNERS ARE RELATIVES, OTHERS ARE PROFESSIONALS HIRED FOR THE FUNERAL.

PREPARING BATA FOR BURIAL

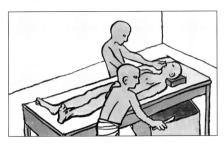

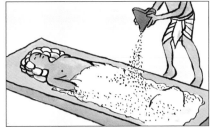

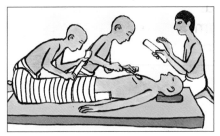

Men called embalmers try to preserve Bata's body for the afterlife. They remove his brains and some internal organs. Then they clean his body and fill it with sweet-smelling spices.

Next, they cover Bata's body with a kind of salt called natron. Bags of natron are packed around his head. Then the body is left for many days until all the moisture left in it has dried out.

Bata's body is wrapped in linen bandages to make a "mummy". He is coated with oils and decorated with jewels and charms. A mask goes over Bata's face. Then he is wrapped again.

BATA'S BODY WAS TAKEN TO THE TOMB IN A BOAT.

THE BOAT WAS PULLED BY OXEN.

SLAVES CARRYING JEWELS, FURNITURE AND FOOD FOR BATA TO ENJOY IN HIS AFTERLIFE.

THE WORLD OF THE SPIRITS

Egyptian people believe in a life after death in which they will work, eat and drink just as they did on earth. Their tombs will be their homes, so wealthy people like Bata's parents take great care preparing their tombs.

Dead people must eat too, so piles of food are painted on tomb walls. People believe that the painted food will, by magic, stop them from being hungry.

Nakht is talking to his children about Bata's death, and his life after death in the world of the spirits.

When Bata died, his soul left his body in the shape of a bird. During the daytime, it flies back to the land of the living to revisit the places Bata knew when he was alive.

A MAP OF THE WORLD OF THE SPIRITS

Wealthy Egyptians have books, called Books of the Dead, put in their tombs. The books contain drawings of the Fields of Yaru – the Egyptian heaven. It is a peaceful land of fields, marshes and canals. After death, good people live there among the gods. They have to work in the fields. To avoid this, rich Egyptians put small statues called *ushabtis* in their tombs. They believe that the *ushabtis* will do the hard work for them.

RA, GOD OF THE SUN

Egyptians believe that each day the Sun travels across the sky in a boat guided by Ra, the falcon-headed god of the Sun. At night, Ra gets into another boat to sail with the Sun through the world of the spirits.

THE SUN

RA

ATA'S TRIP TO THE UNDERWORLD

2

...kht tells his children about the ...ghtening ordeal that dead Bata must ...ce. Before he can live again in the ...orld of the spirits, he must stand trial ...fore Osiris, Lord of the Underworld. ...ly good people pass Osiris's test; the ...st face a terrible fate.

The kingdom of Osiris lies in the West, where the Sun sets. The dead Bata has to travel there by boat. The snake goddess Meresger will go with him to protect him from serpents he may meet in the underworld.

To reach Osiris, Bata has to pass many gateways. Each one is guarded by animal-headed gods. These gods hold knives or feathers. The feathers represent truth. To pass through the gates, Bata must recite magic words written in his Book of the Dead.

BATA

ANUBIS

THOTH

THE DEVOURER

... the judgement hall, which is called ...e Hall of the Two Truths, the dead ...ta will meet Osiris. In front of Osiris ...d 42 judges, Bata must deny that he ...d any wrong in his life.

Jackal-headed Anubis is the god of the Dead. He will test Bata's claim by placing Bata's heart on a set of scales. On the other side of the scales, he places a feather of truth.

If Bata's heart is heavier than the feather, it means he has lied, and a beast called the Devourer will eat him. The beast is part lion, part crocodile and part hippopotamus.

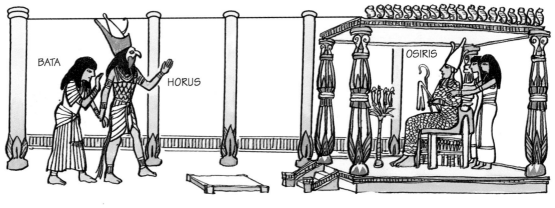

BATA

HORUS

OSIRIS

...is-headed Thoth, the ...ribe of the gods, will ...te down the result of ...e trial. If it proves that ...ta was a good man, ...e will be taken by the ...lcon-headed god ...rus to the throne of ...siris, to worship him. ...en, at last, Bata's ...w life in the Fields ...f Yaru will begin.

THE STORY OF THE PHARAOHS

The story begins in about 3100 BC, when Menes, a king from the south of Egypt (known as Upper Egypt) conquered the north of Egypt (known as Lower Egypt). He built a new capital city at Memphis, and ruled as the first of the Pharaohs.

MENES FIGHTS TO UNITE EGYPT

The first great pyramid was built 400 years later. It was a tomb for Pharaoh Zoser. Before this, Pharaohs were buried in flat-topped tombs called *mastabas*. Zoser's tomb looked like six *mastabas* on top of each other, and is known as the Step Pyramid.

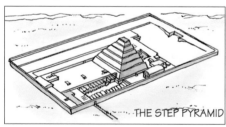
THE STEP PYRAMID

All the great pyramids were built over the next 400 years. The two biggest were built at Giza.

THE GREAT PYRAMIDS

The period when the pyramids were built is known as the Old Kingdom. Egypt was peaceful and grew rich. Peasants farmed the land and priests prayed, to the gods. The rich nobles served their Pharaoh, looked after their lands, and enjoyed hunting.

HUNTING

The nobles finally brought the Old Kingdom to an end. They grew so powerful that they no longer respected the Pharaohs at all. The country split in two and was ruled by rival kings, one in southern Egypt and one in the north.

WARRIORS

This unrest lasted for more than 150 years. It ended when a family who ruled Thebes managed to reunite the country. They crushed all opposition to their rule, and put Thebans in important government positions. They succeeded in restoring peace and limiting the power of the nobles. This new period of calm and prosperity is called the Middle Kingdom.

The Middle Kingdom was another great period for Egypt. Fine hieroglyphic writings were composed. Trading abroad increased. In the Delta and Nubia, chains of great fortresses were built to guard Egypt's borders. Marshes were drained in the Faiyum.

A FORTRESS

After 250 years of peace, civil war broke out again. Upper and Lower Egypt split. Foreigners, known as the Hyksos, conquered Lower Egypt. They used new weapons, including horses and chariots.

THE HYKSOS ATTACK

After a century, the rulers of Upper Egypt drove out the Hyksos. Thebes became the capital of a reunited Egypt. The Theban Pharaoh won back the country's earlier frontiers. Inside Egypt, order was restored.

During the first century of the New Kingdom, Egypt had its first truly powerful woman ruler. She was called Hatshepsut. At first, she ruled Egypt on behalf of her young stepson Tuthmosis III. Then she took all the power of a Pharaoh for herself. She ruled well for 20 years, and built a temple into the cliff face at Deir el Bahari, as a monument to herself.

DEIR EL BAHARI

As soon as Tuthmosis III took power, he tried to wipe out the memory of the woman who had stolen his throne. Then, he attacked Egypt's enemies abroad. In over 15 campaigns he built an empire that stretched from Syria to the Sudan.

TUTHMOSIS II

The empire survived until the end of the reign of Tuthmosis's great-grandson, Amenophis III. It crumbled under Amenophis's son, Akhenaten. He was the most revolutionary of Egypt's Pharaohs. He moved the capital of Egypt from Thebes to a new city which he called Akhetaten.

Above all, he tried to overthrow the old gods, and to replace them with only one god – Aten, the Sun's disc.

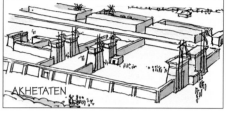
AKHETATEN

Akhenaten's efforts were in vain. During the reign of Tutankhamun, people began to worship all the other gods again. When Tutankhamun died at only 20 years old, his successors did their best to wipe Akhenaten's name from people's memories.

TUTANKHAMUN

Since Amenophis III's reign, Egypt's enemies abroad had been growing stronger. The last rulers of the New Kingdom struggled to keep them in check. After a long war, Rameses II signed a treaty with the Hittites, a people from what is now Turkey. In a great naval battle, Rameses III defeated the Sea Peoples of the Mediterranean.

RAMESES III'S BATTLE AT SEA

After Rameses III's death, Egypt was attacked by different groups of invaders. First came the Nubians and then the Assyrians sacked Thebes in 661 BC.

The Persians conquered Egypt next. The Egyptians hated the Persian people so much that when Alexander the Great of Greece invaded Egypt and defeated them, he was welcomed as a hero.

THE PERSIANS ATTACKING

After Alexander died, one of his generals, Ptolemy, took power. His family ruled Egypt for the next 300 years. Finally, Egypt became part of the Roman Empire. The last of the Pharaohs was Cleopatra. She killed herself with the venom of snake, rather than be ruled by the Roman Octavian.

CLEOPATRA DYING

The Ancient Egyptian way of life gradually disappeared. But its heritage has given much to the modern world, from building and farming to writing and science.

HOW WE KNOW ABOUT ANCIENT EGYPT

After Egypt became a part of the Roman Empire in 30 BC, its old way of life gradually came to an end. People began to worship new gods, and the secrets of hieroglyphic writing were forgotten. The old temples and palaces became ruins, and were covered with sand and rubble.

In the 18th century, Europeans visited Egypt and explored the ruined buildings. People eventually found out how to read hieroglyphic writing again.

Archeologists began to dig up the temples and tombs. They found wall paintings, scrolls and lots of objects used in daily life. People have used all these discoveries to build up a picture of how the Ancient Egyptians lived.

When archeologists found the temple of Abu Simbel, shown above, the great statues of Rameses II, for whom it was built, were covered in sand. The Europeans often damaged buildings when they were looking for treasure. Some even opened tombs with battering rams. Many things were taken back to Europe, like the sculpture of Rameses II shown below.

HOW THE HIEROGLYPHIC CODE WAS CRACKED

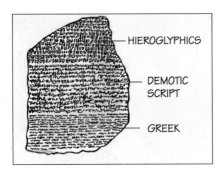

HIEROGLYPHICS

DEMOTIC SCRIPT

GREEK

The vital clue to the meaning of hieroglyphs was a stone dug up in 1799, near Rosetta, in the Delta. A message was written on it in Greek and in two kinds of Egyptian writing, demotic and hieroglyphic.

A French scholar called Jean-François Champollion compared the hieroglyphs with the Greek text, which he understood. He worked for 14 years before he made out the meaning of a single word.

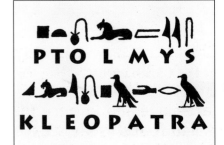

PTOLMYS

KLEOPATRA

The first word he recognized was "Ptolemy", which was the name of the Greek Pharaohs. By comparing it with the spelling of "Cleopatra", he worked out the symbols for the letters "p", "l" and "o".

TUTANKHAMUN'S TOMB

The greatest discovery in the history of Egyptian archeology was finding the tomb of the young king Tutankhamun. Most of the pharaoh's treasure was still inside the tomb, because grave robbers had been unable to find it.

The discovery was made by an English archeologist named Howard Carter. From what he knew about royal tombs, he was sure that there must still be one undiscovered tomb in the area known as the Valley of the Kings.

For five years he searched without finding anything. Then, on November 4, 1922, workers uncovered the first step of a flight of stone stairs while digging under a group of huts.

Carter and a colleague uncovering the entrance to Tutankhamun's tomb

Carter guessed at once that they had found what they had been looking for. Three weeks after the first step had been unearthed, Carter and his men uncovered the entrance to Pharaoh Tutankhamun's tomb.

Carter made an opening in the wall blocking the burial rooms and looked inside. Holding a candle through the hole, he peered into the darkness. "Can you see anything?" someone asked. "Yes", Carter replied. "Wonderful things."

Carter looking into Tutankhamun's burial chamber

Carter said that he could see "strange animals, statues and gold – everywhere the glint of gold." In the middle of the main room was a golden couch, shaped like a cow.

The archeologists found over 2,000 objects stored in four separate rooms. Many of them were made of gold. The mummy of the king's body was discovered inside a magnificent coffin.

Tutankhamun's body was found inside this golden coffin.

INDEX

ACKNOWLEDGEMENTS

This book was prepared in consultation with W.V. Davies,
Assistant Keeper of Egyptian Antiquities for the British Museum,
and Dr. Anne Millard, author of several books
and articles on Ancient Egypt for children.
Thanks to Rachael Swann and Mark Swift
Tutankhamun's coffin (page 31) artwork by Ian Jackson